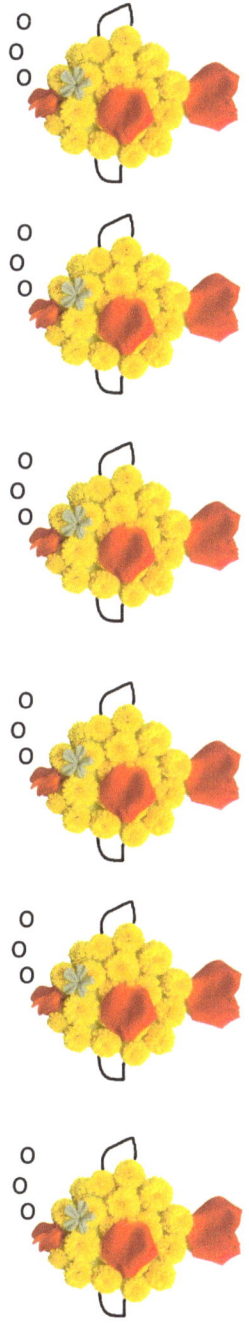

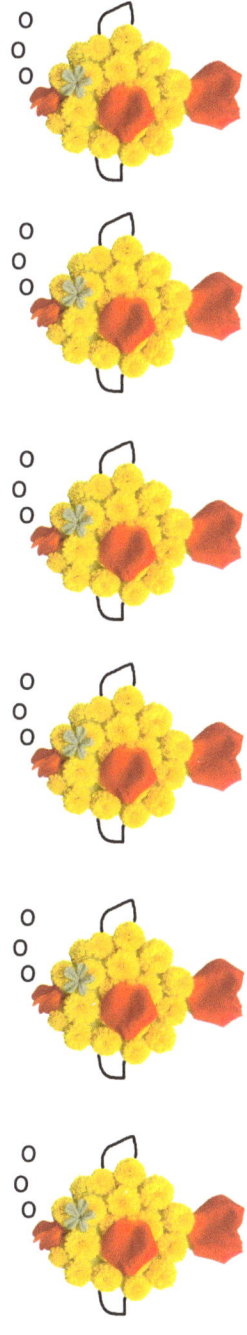

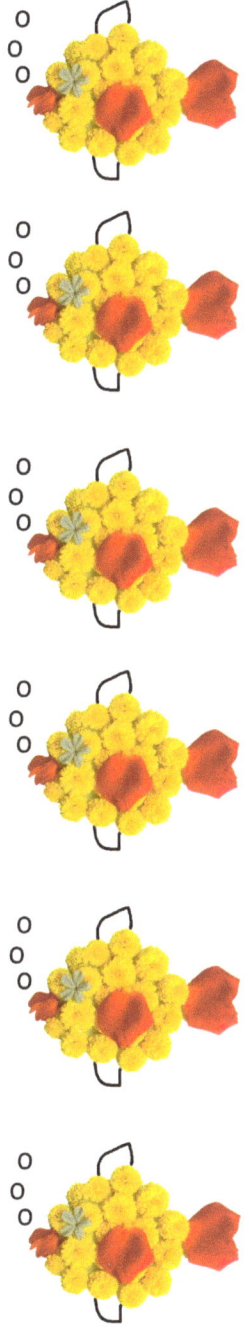

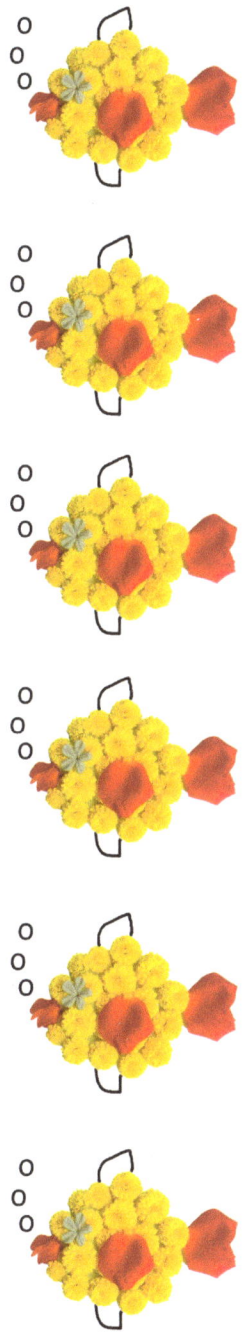

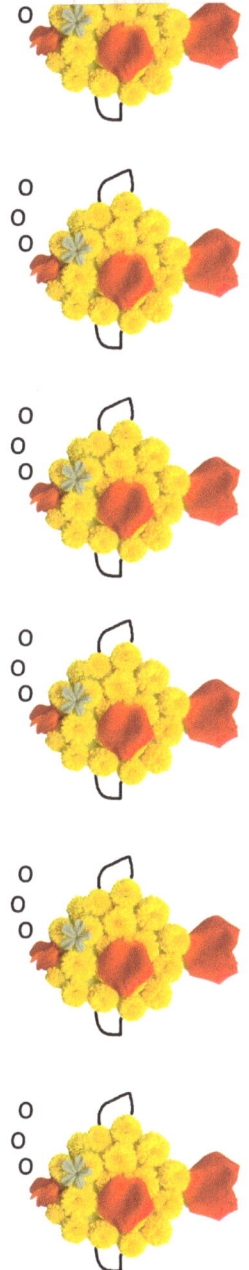

For my faithful friends,
Kimberly, Ann, Amy, and Kacy.

H.P. Gentileschi Publishing House
Austin - Rome

www.hpgentileschi.com

Is this a fish?
No! This is a frog.

Is this a fish?
No! This is a fan.

Is this a fish?
No! This is a fruit.

Is this a fish?
No! This is a five.

Is this a fish?
No! This is a flamingo.

Is this a fish?
No! This is a family.

Is this a fish?
No! This is a foot.

Is this a fish?
No! This is a fly.

Is this a fish?
No! This is a face.

Is this a fish?
Yes! This is a fish!

words in this book:

fish

foot

fan

five

face

fruit

frog

fly

flamingo

Make collage art with real flowers!

First, draw an outline of your design with a black marker on a white sheet of paper. Then gather fresh flowers to arrange on top. When you have finished, take a photograph of your work!

You can also make a picture with photographs of flowers!

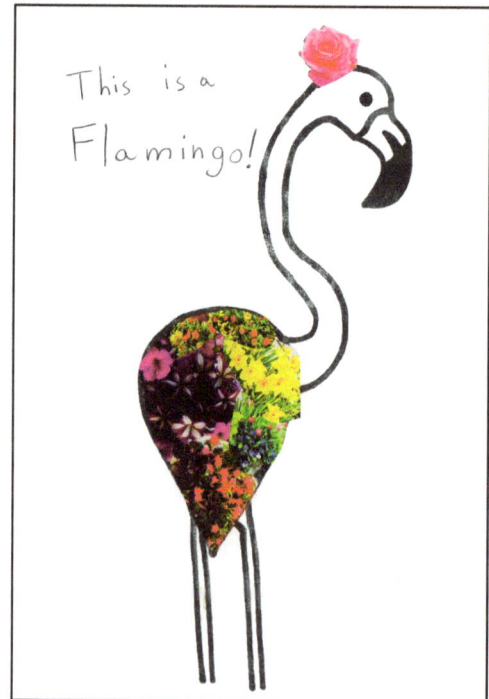

This is a Flamingo!

F

Twirl your finger as if it's following
a swimming fish in a bowl, and say:
"f, f, fish"

UDL and H.P. Gentileschi

At H.P. Gentileschi Publishing House, we create all our books and resources using the Universal Design for Learning (UDL) inclusive principle. The goal of UDL is to provide multiple means of teaching methods and materials to remove any barriers to learning and give all children equal opportunities to grow.

For this reason, you will find our books in numerous media forms:
- In print on paperback with easy-to-read fonts and not overly busy illustrations
- Digital eBooks on Amazon Kindle
- Audiobooks linked to each book with QR codes

Our books also come with fun experiential learning activities, such as Letter Actions and craft projects that provide physical movement options that reinforce the book's teaching objectives.

These UDL resources can be helpful for all kids, including English Language Learners and kids with diverse learning and attention abilities. Our book and curriculum characters represent the beautiful diversity that is found in our world, so every child feels included.

AlphaBOX Book Series

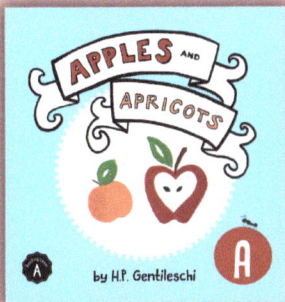

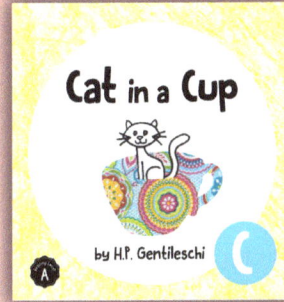

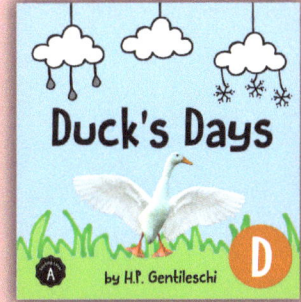

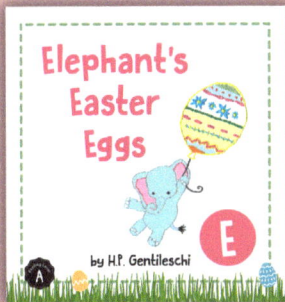

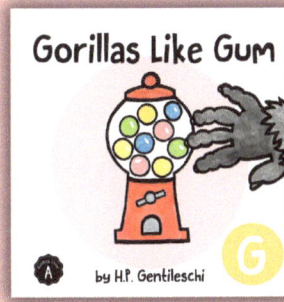

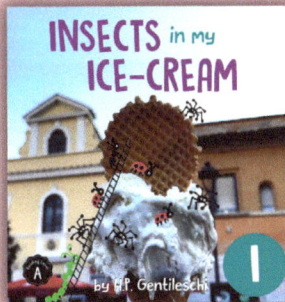

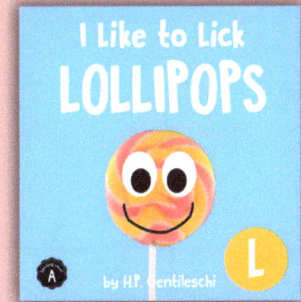

Apples and Apricots by H.P. Gentileschi — A

Boy on a Bus by H.P. Gentileschi — B

Cat in a Cup by H.P. Gentileschi — C

Duck's Days by H.P. Gentileschi — D

Elephant's Easter Eggs by H.P. Gentileschi — E

Is This a Fish? by H.P. Gentileschi — F

Gorillas Like Gum by H.P. Gentileschi — G

This Hand by H.P. Gentileschi — H

INSECTS in my ICE-CREAM by H.P. Gentileschi — I

When Do You Drink Juice? by H.P. Gentileschi — J

WHERE IS KATE'S KEY? by H.P. Gentileschi — K

I Like to Lick LOLLIPOPS by H.P. Gentileschi — L

MILK in My Mailbox
by H.P. Gentileschi
M

Does a nut have a nose?
by H.P. Gentileschi
N

ONE OCTOPUS in the OLIVE TREE
by H.P. Gentileschi
O

Penguin's Paper Plane
by H.P. Gentileschi
P

The Queen's Question
by H.P. Gentileschi
Q

Rabbit's Rainbow in Rome
R

Snake's Snacks
by H.P. Gentileschi
S

Does a Tomato Have Teeth?
by H.P. Gentileschi
T

Under My Umbrella
by H.P. Gentileschi
U

Victoria's Violin
by H.P. Gentileschi
V

The Whale in the Water
by H.P. Gentileschi
W

Fox has a Box
by H.P. Gentileschi
X

Your Yellow Yo-Yo
by H.P. Gentileschi
Y

Zero Zebras in the ZOO!
by H.P. Gentileschi
Z

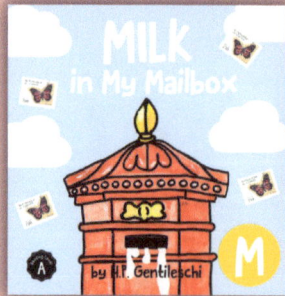

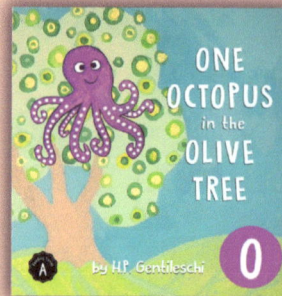

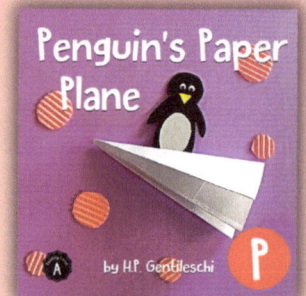

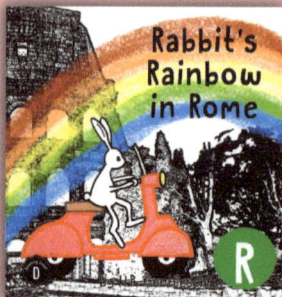

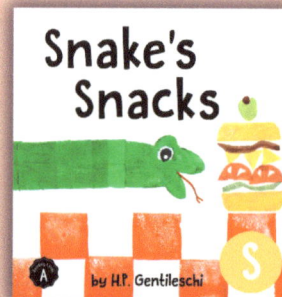

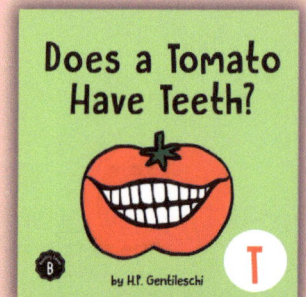

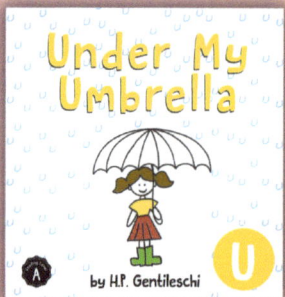

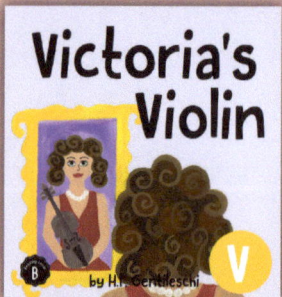

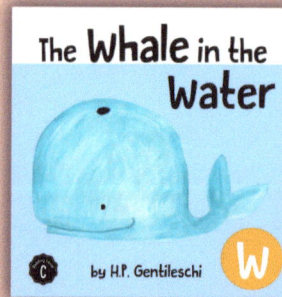

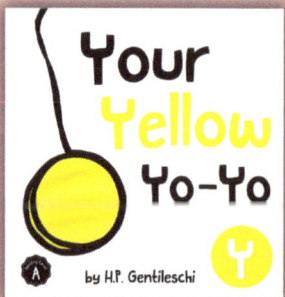

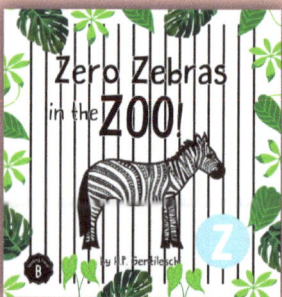

H.P. Gentileschi
Publishing House
www.HPgentileschi.com

For all of our Letter Name actions, visit our website!
www.hpgentileschi.com

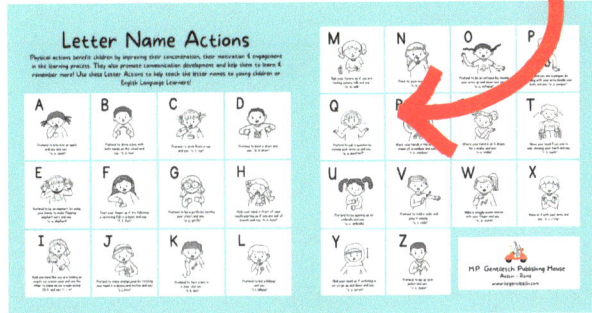

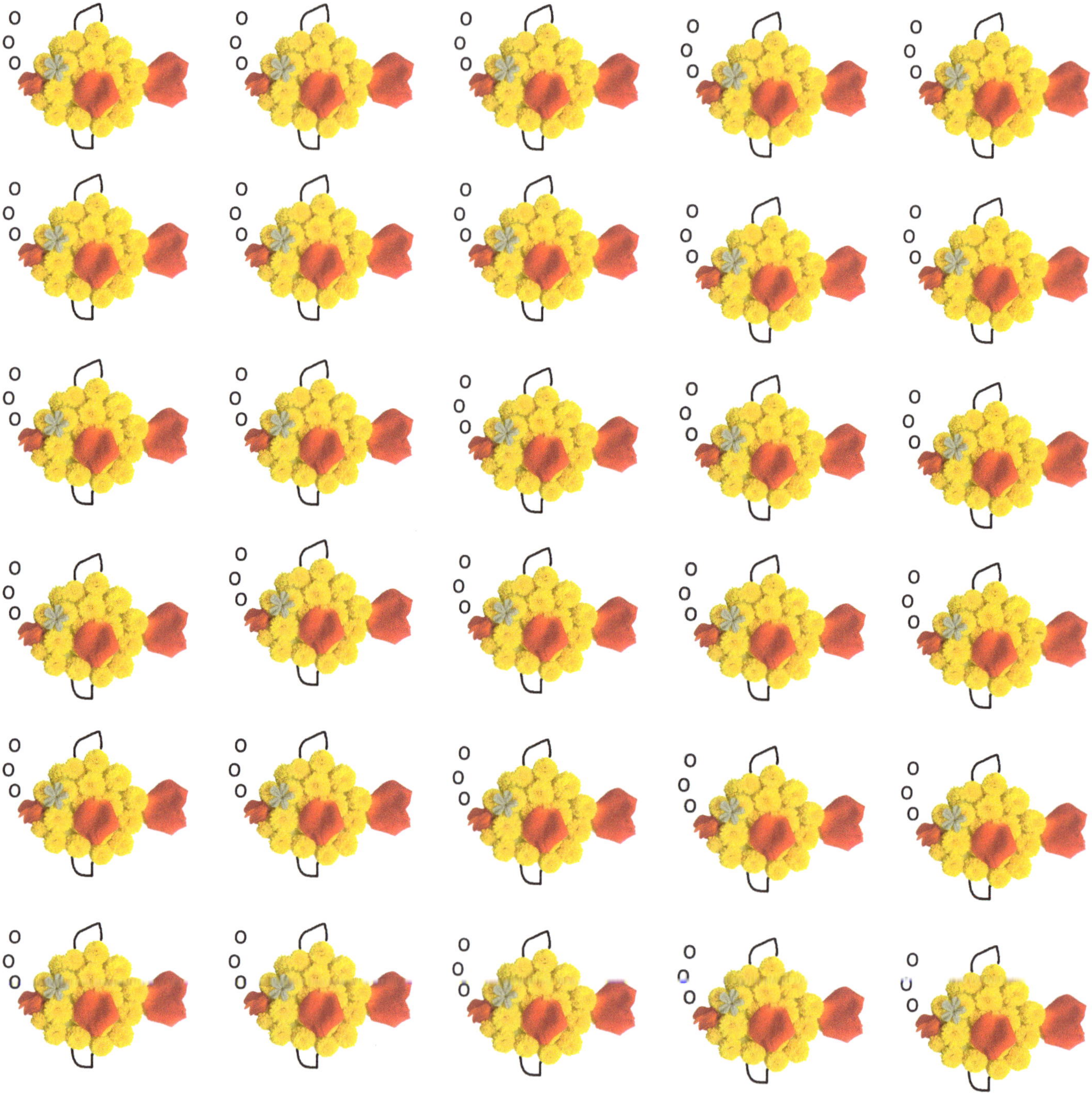

www.ingramcontent.com/pod-product-compliance
Lightning Source LLC
Chambersburg PA
CBHW040232070426
42447CB00030B/236

9 781948 023054